Oh Coward!

Devised and Directed
by Roderick Cook

Doubleday & Company, Inc.
Garden City, New York

Oh Coward!

A Musical Comedy Revue

by Noël Coward

iv

To Sir, with Love

Life needn't be grey,
Although it's changing day by day,
Though a few old dreams may decay,
Play, orchestra, play . . .

Acknowledgments

Oh Coward! was first presented in New York at the New Theatre on October 4, 1972. It was produced by Wroderick Productions, directed by Roderick Cook and starred Barbara Cason, Roderick Cook, and Jamie Ross. The musical direction and arrangements were by Rene Wiegert (additional arrangements by Herbert Helbig and Nicholas Deutsch). The setting was designed by Herbert Senn and Helen Pond, with lighting by James Nisbet Clark.

The production stage manager was Jay Leo Colt, assisted by William Lee Martis. The orchestra included Uel Wade, Bernard Karl, and Richard Cook.

The producer wishes to thank Gino Empry, Jay Kramer, Geoffrey Johnson, and Richard Seader for their assistance with the production, and Angela Leigh, Piers Gilson, and George Bunt for their contributions.

Foreword

OH COWARD! first saw the lights on May 14, 1970, at the Theatre in the Dell, Toronto, Canada. It was then titled *A Noël Coward Revue, or To Sir, With Love*. Its story goes backwards and forwards from there.

It was five years earlier, in 1965, that I had first broached the idea to the Master. At this time, people had just begun to re-examine the musical treasure chests of Cole Porter, Rodgers and Hart, George and Ira Gershwin, Jerome Kern, etc., and some of the uncut gems they found there were being set on stages, and attracting a lot of customers. Obviously something was in the air. And it was spring . . .

Dear Noël, I wrote. *Look, stop me if you've heard it, but . . .* and went on to outline the idea of a musical revue, composed entirely of his words and music, some well-known, some obscure, to be devised and directed by me. It could open, I said, in a cabaret theatre in Canada, where I was currently enjoying a success with another revue, and, assuming all went well, could transfer to some modest house in New York later the same season. Just like that. Not being an intimate friend of Mr. Coward's at that time (our first-name acquaintanceship had sprung up as a result of my appearing as a slightly distraught diplomat in his last Broadway musical *The Girl Who Came to Supper*), it would have been very easy for him to have dismissed the idea, with typical charm and politeness, as sheer sauce.

To my immense surprise, I had an answer back within the week. *Dear Roddy, What a lovely idea! Send me a dummy programme and let's talk.*

Having anticipated at least a month's delay before hearing anything at all, this lightning rejoinder put me on the spot. I had no dummy programme. I had only the vaguest notion of a show. All I did have was a list of ninety-seven numbers down on paper, almost daring me to make a running order. The plot thinned.

It was a cold Thursday in Toronto, and raining. I glared at the titles I had selected. They were variously famous, infamous, or unknown: witty, charming, sad, funny, lyrical, savage, graceful, and downright vulgar: I loved them all. But how was I to confess to their author that, after all, I hadn't the remotest idea how to shape them into an evening's entertainment? I glared at them again, till they began to dance before my eyes. Where was the thread, the theme? Chronology? Boring. A musical history? Pretentious. The Life and Times of . . . ? Interminable. And then God, or somebody, sat on my shoulder and pointed: "Look! How about putting 'London Pride' with 'Stately Homes' and making a thing about England . . . and look at all those women! 'Nina,' 'Mrs. Wentworth-Brewster' . . . and what about all those oom-pah-pah tunes that Noël has loved since a child—there's a Music Hall medley there . . ."

I am not for one moment pretending that the stainless steel construction of this simple but elegant show was revealed to me in a manner resembling the Eleventh Commandment; what I am suggesting is that, impelled by a direct, sudden and possibly remunerative opportunity, the heart *can* find its reasons, even unto that of the First Act closing. Let alone the Second Act dance divertissement.

Whereupon, the entire idea went down the drain.

There were squabbles in Canada and the producers parted company. Months passed. Six separate impresarios in New York took up the idea enthusiastically but later put it down again, regretfully. Years passed. Some British producers were mildly intrigued, but remained non-committal. It seemed, at this point, as if the whole idea of a Noël Coward Retrospective had whirled itself to a stand-still. Everybody thought it was a brilliant idea, but nobody knew what to do with it. Among the dear, talented people who also expressed regrets at this time were Brian Bedford and Tammy Grimes (who later had a great success on Broadway in *Private Lives*), Patricia Routledge and Wendy Toye (who both contributed to a later London revue *Cowardy Custard*), and in 1968 (the year of *Hair*), George Grizzard, Dorothy Loudon, Carole Shelley, Arthur Mitchell, Tom Kneebone, and Bonnie Schon bared their all on Broadway in a bastardisation of the original concept, called *Noël Coward's Sweet Potato,* wherein "Don't Put Your Daughter on the Stage, Mrs. Worthington" was sung as a rock ballad by a renegade priest, and the Balcony Scene from *Private Lives* was done on roller skates. Clive Barnes said that the whole thing seemed to be aimed at "the middle-aged in heart" and the show closed in weeks.

But then, two years later, the middle-aged struck back. In 1970, nostalgia was "in" in New York, and in London, Noël Coward was top of the heap again. The new National Theatre had presented an all-star revival of *Hay Fever* directed by the author in its very first season of World Classics, and everyone on the South Bank was beside himself with joy and merriment, and the West End chortled happily. On New Year's Day, 1970, it was announced that Mr. Coward was now officially "Sir Noël"—and what is laughingly known as "The Coward Revival" had reached a peak, in Britain.

Meanwhile, back in the Commonwealth . . . I happened to be in Toronto again, talking vaguely of doing another revue, when suddenly the idea of a Coward show came up again. This time the moment seemed to be right, and within weeks I had the old show whittled back into shape, secured Tom Kneebone as my partner and co-star, enlisted Dinah Christie as our leading lady, and we became an instant Smash Hit.

So much for our story backwards . . .

Forwards, we proceeded to break all performance records in Canadian theatre history (we ran longer than *Hair*). We then died a slow death for three months in Chicago. We lurked in Boston for a very chilly six weeks. But I wanted to bring it home, to New York, before I let it go for good— and with a lot of help from my friends (old ones like Rene Wiegert, Helen Pond, and Herbert Senn and new ones like Barbara Cason, Jamie Ross) I was able to do just that. The Opening Night was a dream, and as for the Gala Performance, honoring the author . . .

Enough. Thank you for caring sufficiently about *Oh Coward!* to want to see how it is done. Here are the facts, in this book. The imagination and love are up to you.

RODERICK COOK

New York City
1973

While the above was being prepared for publication, we received the news that Noël Coward had died peacefully in his sleep at his home in Jamaica. *Oh Coward!* was the last show of his that he ever saw, and everyone concerned with that performance will give eternal thanks that we were all able to show him, in person, through his own words and music (and, as he himself would have said, "in the *nick* of time") how very much we loved and admired him. "I do not approve of mourning," he once remarked, "I approve only of remembering." Remembering Noël will not be difficult, for while there is still a reason for singing and laughter in this world, he will always be with us.

R.C.

Act One

INTERMISSION

Act Two

xvi

Act One

Introduction

As the Overture begins, the lights dim up on the permanent stage setting, which suggests a Victorian toy theatre, with a gaily decorated proscenium arch and rich red velvet curtains. Featured in a spotlight is a caricature of Noël Coward impersonating the masks of Comedy and Tragedy, with a cigarette holder clenched firmly between his teeth.

After the Overture, the theatre lights dim completely. From the darkness comes the far-off sound of a piano—a child practising five-finger exercises.

Pin spots pick out the faces of the three performers.

"The Boy Actor" (from *Not Yet the Dodo* and Other Verses)

JAMIE

     I can remember. I can remember.
The months of November and December
     Were filled for me with peculiar joys
So different from those of other boys

1

BARBARA

  For other boys would be counting the days
Until end of term and holiday times
  But I was acting in Christmas plays
While they were taken to pantomimes.

RODERICK

  I never cared who scored the goal
Or which side won the silver cup,
  I never learnt to bat or bowl
But I heard—the curtain going up.

A faint fanfare from the orchestra. The lights brighten.

JAMIE

That was Noël Coward, writing about his own childhood.

RODERICK

And for the next sixty years, Noël Coward heard the curtain
going up . . .

BARBARA

And up . . .

JAMIE

And up . . .

BARBARA

And up . . .

RODERICK

And up . . . until, as he himself once said "It created a posi-
tive draught."

BARBARA

So tonight, we'd like to give you some idea of what went
on while the curtain was up . . .

JAMIE

In words and music by—The Master!

The curtains open.

Oh Coward!

The opening medley is sung and danced on the full stage by the whole company.

"Something to Do with Spring" (from WORDS AND MUSIC)

   ALL
The sun is shining where clouds have been—
Maybe it's something to do with Spring.
   BARBARA
I feel no older than seventeen—
   JAMIE *and* RODERICK
Maybe it's something to do with Spring.
   JAMIE
A something I can't express,
   RODERICK
A kind[1] of lilt in the air,
   ALL
A lyrical loveliness,
Seems everywhere.

That sheep's behaviour is just[2] obscene
JAMIE *and* RODERICK
Maybe it's something to do with,
ALL
Some crazy something to do with,
Maybe it's something to do with Spring.
Spring!
Ring-a-ding![3]

"Bright Young People"
(from COCHRAN'S 1931 REVUE)

JAMIE
Look at us three
Representatives we
Of a nation renowned for virility.
BARBARA
We've formed a cult of puerility
Just for fun.
RODERICK
You may deplore
The effects of war
That are causing the world to decay a bit.
BARBARA
We've found our place and will play a bit
In the sun.
JAMIE
Though Waterloo was won upon the playing fields of Eton,
BARBARA
The next war will be photographed, and lost,

4

RODERICK
By Cecil Beaton.
ALL
Bright young people,
Ready to do and to dare
JAMIE
We casually strive
To keep London alive
From Chelsea to Bloomsbury Square.
RODERICK
We give lovely parties that last through the night,
BARBARA
I dress as a woman and scream with delight,
JAMIE
We wake up at lunch time and find we're still tight.
ALL
What could be duller than that?[4]

ALL
Bright young people,
JAMIE
Don't think our lives are not full.
BARBARA
I make little hats
From Victorian mats
RODERICK
And I work with tinfoil and wool.
JAMIE
Our critics are often excessively rude,
To one of my portraits they always allude:
It's me, worked in beads, upside down, in the nude.
RODERICK *and* BARBARA
What could be duller than that?

JAMIE

Psychology experts we often perplex

RODERICK

And doctors have warned us we'll end up as wrecks.

BARBARA

But they get a degree if they find out our sex.

ALL

What could be duller than that?[5]

"Poor Little Rich Girl"
   (from ON WITH THE DANCE)

RODERICK *and* JAMIE

Poor little rich girl,
You're a bewitched girl,
Better beware!

JAMIE

Laughing at danger,

RODERICK

Virtue a stranger,

RODERICK *and* JAMIE

Better take care!

JAMIE

The life you lead sets all your nerves a-jangle,

RODERICK

Your love affairs are in a hopeless tangle,

RODERICK *and* JAMIE

Though you're a child, dear,
Your life's a wild typhoon,
In lives of leisure
The craze for pleasure
Steadily grows.

6

BARBARA
Cocktails and laughter,
RODERICK *and* JAMIE
But what comes after?
Nobody knows.
You're weaving love into a mad jazz pattern,
Ruled by Pantaloon.
Poor little rich girl, don't drop a stitch too soon.

"Zigeuner" (from BITTER SWEET)

BARBARA
Play to me beneath the summer moon
Zigeuner!—Zigeuner!—Zigeuner!
All I ask of life is just to listen
To the songs that you sing,
My spirit like a bird on the wing
Your melodies adoring—soaring . . .

"Let's Say Goodbye" (from WORDS AND MUSIC)

RODERICK
Let's look on love as a plaything.
All these sweet moments we've known
Then, without forgetting happiness that has passed,
There'll be no regretting
Fun—that didn't quite last . . .[6]

"This Is a Changing World"
(from Pacific 1860)

    JAMIE
This is a changing world, my dear,
New songs are sung—new dawns appear,
Though we grow older year by year
Our hearts can still be gay,
    ALL
Where are the snows of yesteryear?
When winter's gone and spring is here
    JAMIE
No regrets are worth a tear,
    ALL
We're living in a changing world, my dear . . .[7]

"We Were Dancing" (from "We Were Dancing"
—Tonight at 8:30)

    RODERICK
We were dancing
    RODERICK *and* JAMIE
And the gods must have found it entrancing
For they smiled
On this moment undefiled
    ALL
By the care and woe
That mortals know.
We were dancing

And the music and lights were enhancing
Our desire,
When the world caught on fire,
You and I were . . .

"Dance Little Lady"
(from THIS YEAR OF GRACE!)

RODERICK
Dance, dance, dance little lady
Youth is fleeting—to the rhythm beating
In your mind
JAMIE
Dance, dance, dance little lady
So obsessed with second best,
No rest you'll ever find,
BARBARA
Time and tide and trouble
Never, never wait
Let the cauldron bubble
Justify your fate.
Dance, dance, dance little lady
Dance, dance, dance little lady
Dance, dance, dance little lady
Dance . . .
Dance . . .

"A Room with a View"
(from THIS YEAR OF GRACE!)

RODERICK
A room with a view—and you,
And[8] no one to worry us,

BARBARA
No one to hurry us—through
This dream we've found,

JAMIE
We'll gaze at the sky—and try
To guess what it's all about,

ALL
Then we will figure out—why
The world is round.
We'll be as happy and contented
As birds upon a tree,
High above the mountains and the sea.

RODERICK *and* JAMIE
We'll bill and we'll coo

ALL
Oo—oo

RODERICK *and* JAMIE
And sorrow will never come,

BARBARA
Oh, will it ever come—true?

ALL
Our room . . .

"Sail Away" (from ACE OF CLUBS and SAIL AWAY)

BARBARA

When your life gets⁹ too difficult to rise above,
Sail away—

RODERICK *and* JAMIE

Sail away—

BARBARA

Sail away—

RODERICK *and* JAMIE

Sail away.

JAMIE

When your heart feels as dreary as a worn-out glove,
Sail away—

RODERICK *and* BARBARA

Sail away—

JAMIE

Sail away.

ALL

But when soon or late
You recognize your fate,
That will be your great, great day,
On the wings of the morning with your own true love,
Sail away—
Sail away—
Sail away!

The music builds to a big crescendo and the lights fade.

England

"London Pastoral" (from *Ashes of Roses*— "Star Quality")

JAMIE *is discovered, downstage, carrying a raincoat and an umbrella*

There is much to recommend London—particularly Hyde Park—on a sunny afternoon in spring, when the grass is newly green, and there is a feeling of lightness in the air.

Subconsciously affected by this, the most prosaic citizens frequently give way to a certain abandon. Fathers of families take off their coats and waistcoats and lie on their backs, gazing up at the sky. Their wives sit near them, keeping an eye on the children and allowing the sun to burn semicircular areas of pink on to their necks.

Younger people lie unashamedly close, sometimes asleep, sometimes lazily awake, murmuring laconically to each other, sucking sweets, smoking cigarettes, relaxed and content, soothed into a sensual lassitude by the promise in the air and the gentle weather.

As a general rule, decorum is observed—although occasionally passion flames suddenly between them and they lie, legs and arms entwined, oblivious of passers-by, lost in brief ecstasy.

Police constables regulate these transient excesses with admirable discretion. Nothing is allowed to get out of control. The decencies are upheld. The birds sing (*the theme of "London Pride" is heard quietly in the background*) and the cries of children, the barking of dogs, the far-off strains of a military band, together with the incessant rumble of traffic in the distance, all provide a muted orchestration to this unremarkable—but at the same time, unique—London Pastoral.[10]

The lights fade on JAMIE *and pick up immediately on* RODERICK *and* BARBARA.

"That Is the End of the News" (from SIGH NO MORE)

RODERICK *and* BARBARA *enter wearing heavy coats, scarves, hats, etc. and carrying streamers, rattles and various objects suggesting that they have just come from the local football field. They are deeply depressed.*
Music plays quietly in the background.

RODERICK
Come on, Beryl—we're going to miss that bloomin' bus . . .

BARBARA
All right all right—I'm doin' the best I can—my feet are fair frozen . . .

RODERICK
Your feet are frozen . . . that whole bloody football team had its feet frozen . . .

13

BARBARA

Oh, come, Fred—it were a fair game . . .

RODERICK

Fair game? Fair game? Twenty-two frozen feet trying to play football?

BARBARA

Oh, don't take it so hard, love—they did get one goal.

RODERICK

One goal . . . yes, that's what they got—one goal—one of their men fell over laughing—kicked the ball into his own net!

BARBARA

Well, we'll be 'ome soon—have a nice cuppa tea and a sit-down . . . if I ever sit down again; oh my bum's numb, too . . .

RODERICK

Now where is that bus . . .

BARBARA

I do hope we haven't missed it . . .

RODERICK

Oh, my Gawd, so do I. The last time I missed this bus, I had to wait three-quarters of an hour for another. (*Pause*) And a dog bit me.

BARBARA

Oh, come on, Fred—remember, we're British . . . It's bein' so cheerful as keeps us goin' . . .

RODERICK

You're right, Beryl . . . You're not wrong, you're right . . . up at the corners, that's what I say, up at the corners! (*indicating a smile*)[11]

The music brightens and in the course of the number, cheerfulness breaks in.

14

RODERICK *(Sung)*
We are told very loudly and often
To lift up our hearts,
BARBARA
We are told that good humor will soften
Fate's cruellest darts,
BOTH
So however bad our domestic troubles may be
We just shake with amusement and sing with glee.
Heighho,
RODERICK
Mum's got[12] those pains again,
BARBARA
Granny's in bed with her varicose veins again,
RODERICK
Everyone's gay because dear cousin Florrie
Was run down on Saturday night by a lorry,
BARBARA
We're so thrilled, Elsie's miscarriage[13]
Occurred on the Wednesday after her marriage . . .[14]
RODERICK
When Albert fell down
All the steps of the Town Hall
He got three bad cuts and a bruise.
BARBARA
We're delighted
To be able to say
We're unable to pay
Off our debts,
RODERICK
We're excited
Because Rover's[15] got mange
And we've run up a bill at the vet's.

Three cheers

BARBARA

Dear little Sidney
Produced a spectacular stone in his kidney,

RODERICK

Now he's had seven . . .[16]

BARBARA

So God's in his heaven

BOTH

And that is the end of the news.[17]

Music continues under.

RODERICK (*Speaking*)
Now where is that bleedin' bus?

BARBARA

You don't suppose they're on strike again, do you?

RODERICK

Oh my Gawd, I hope not. It was the dockers last week . . .

BARBARA

And the plumbers the week before that . . .

RODERICK

Yeah . . . and the Queen ain't feelin' too hot either.

BARBARA (*Horror-struck*)
Ooh, you are awful . . .[18]

The music brightens again.

BARBARA (*Singing*)
Heighho, what a catastrophy,
Grandfather's brain is beginning to atrophy,

RODERICK

Last Sunday night after eating an apple
He made a rude noise in the Methodist chapel.

BARBARA

Now don't laugh, poor Mrs. Mason
Was washing some smalls in her lavatory basin
When that old corroded
Gas-heater exploded
And blew her smack into the mews.

RODERICK

We've been done in
By that mortgage foreclosure
And father went out on a blind,
He got run in
For indecent exposure
And ever so heavily fined.

BOTH

Heighho hididdle-diddle

RODERICK

Aunt Isabel's shingles have met in the middle,

BARBARA

She's buried in Devon

RODERICK

So God's in His heaven[19]

BOTH

And that is the end of the news!

They are both hysterical with laughter by this time. The bus approaches them but goes straight by.

RODERICK

Aaaaah! We missed it . . .

BARBARA

Oh no . . .

RODERICK

It's all your fault . . .

BARBARA

My fault?

RODERICK

You and your bloody frozen feet . . .[20]

The music drowns the rest of the argument. The lights fade.

"The Stately Homes of England" (from OPERETTE)

JAMIE *and* RODERICK, *in separate spots, downstage*

JAMIE

The Stately Homes of England
We proudly represent,
We only keep them up for
Americans to rent.
Though the pipes that supply the bathroom burst
And the lavatory makes you fear the worst,
It was used by Charles the First
Quite informally,
And later by George the Fourth
On a journey north.
The State Apartments keep their
Historical renown,
It's wiser not to sleep there
In case they tumble down;
But still if they ever catch on fire
Which, with any luck, they might
We'll fight
For the Stately Homes of England.

RODERICK

The Stately Homes of England,
Though rather in the lurch,
Provide a lot of chances
For Psychical Research—
There's the ghost of a crazy younger son
Who murdered, in 1351,
An extremely rowdy Nun
Who resented it
And people who come to call
Meet her in the hall.
The baby in the guest wing,
Who crouches by the grate,
Was walled up in the west wing
In 1428.
And if anyone spots
The Queen of Scots
In a hand-embroidered shroud
We're proud
Of the Stately Homes of England.

BOTH

The Stately Homes of England,
Although a trifle bleak,
Historically speaking,
Are more or less unique.

RODERICK

We've a cousin who won the Golden Fleece

JAMIE

And a very peculiar fowling-piece
Which was sent to Cromwell's niece,

RODERICK

Who detested it,

19

And rapidly sent it back
With a dirty crack.

JAMIE
A note we have from Chaucer
Contains a bawdy joke.

RODERICK
We also have a saucer
That Bloody Mary broke.

JAMIE
We've two pairs of tights
King Arthur's Knights
Had completely worn away.

BOTH
Sing Hey!
For the Stately Homes of England!

The lights black out.

"London Pride" (from UP AND DOING)

The lights dim up slowly on BARBARA, *who carries a small bunch of pink flowers in her hand.*

BARBARA
There's a little city flower every spring unfailing
Growing in the crevices by some London railing,
Though it has a Latin name, in town and countryside
We in England call it London Pride.

London Pride has been handed down to us.
London Pride is a flower that's free.
London Pride means our own dear town to us,

20

And our pride it forever will be.
Whoa Liza,
See the coster barrows,
Vegetable marrows
And the fruit piled high.
Whoa Liza,
Little London sparrows,
Covent Garden Market where the costers cry.
Cockney feet
Mark the beat of history.
Every street
Pins a memory down.
Nothing ever can break or harm
The charm of London Town.[21]

The lights fade slowly.

Family Album

"Auntie Jessie" (circa 1924)

RODERICK (*Spoken*)
We must all be very kind to Auntie Jessie,
For she's never been a Mother or a Wife,
You mustn't throw your toys at her
Or make a vulgar noise at her,
She hasn't led a very happy life.
You must never fill her nightdress case with beetles
Or whip her[22] Horlick's Malted Milk to foam,
Though her kiss is worse than death
It is rude[23] to hold your breath
For Charity, we hope, begins at home.[24]

The lights cross-fade to . . .

"Uncle Harry" (from PACIFIC 1860 and NOËL COWARD IN LAS VEGAS)

As the orchestra strikes up a vaudeville vamp, BARBARA *and* JAMIE *enter.*

JAMIE

Hello, hello, hello . . . hello Barbara . . .

BARBARA

Hello Jamie . . . having a good time?

JAMIE

Very nice, thank you.

BARBARA

It's a pretty theatre, isn't it?

JAMIE

Lovely . . . and a very nice audience too.

BARBARA

Yes they are.

JAMIE

I think we've got the carriage trade in tonight.

BARBARA

Oh ho! (*Indicating backstage*) What was *he* going on about?

JAMIE

His Auntie Jessie.

BARBARA

His Auntie Jessie?

JAMIE

His Auntie Jessie.

BARBARA

His Auntie Jessie! How boring.

JAMIE

Well . . .

The music swells and they sing.

JAMIE

We all of us have relations,[25]

BARBARA

You've heard it a thousand times,[26]

JAMIE

Our relatives were not excessively bright,

BARBARA

They loved to go off on missions
To rather peculiar climes
And lead the wretched heathen to the light.

JAMIE

A few of them got beaten up
In course of these rampages,

BARBARA

My Great-Aunt Maud got eaten up
While singing "Rock of Ages,"

JAMIE

These family obligations
Admittedly are a bore

BARBARA

But there is just one uncle

BOTH

That we positively adore:
Poor Uncle Harry
Wanted to be a missionary
So he took a ship and sailed away.

JAMIE

This visionary

BARBARA

Hotly pursued by dear Aunt Mary,

JAMIE

Found a South Sea isle on which to stay.

BARBARA

The natives treated[27] them kindly
And invited them to dine

JAMIE

On yams and clams and human hams
And vintage coconut wines,

24

BARBARA
The taste of which was filthy—
But the after-effects *divine*.

JAMIE
Poor Uncle Harry
Got a bit gay and longed to tarry,
BARBARA
This, Aunt Mary couldn't quite allow.
JAMIE
She lectured him severely
On a number of church affairs
BARBARA
But when she'd gone to bed,
He made a getaway down the stairs,
JAMIE
For he longed to find the answer
To a few of the maiden's prayers.
BOTH
Uncle Harry's not a missionary now.

BOTH
Poor Uncle Harry
BARBARA
After a chat with dear Aunt Mary
Thought the time had come to make a row.
JAMIE
He lined up all the older girls
In one of the local sheds
BARBARA
And while he was reviling them
And tearing himself to shreds
JAMIE
They took their Mother Hubbards off
And tied them around their heads.

BOTH

Uncle Harry's not a missionary now

BARBARA

He's awfully happy!

BOTH

But he's certainly not a missionary now.

The vaudeville vamp repeats.

JAMIE (*Spoken*)

Second chorus coming right up.

BARBARA (*To the orchestra*)

From the top . . .

They continue singing.

JAMIE

Now Uncle was just a seeker,
A dreamer sincerely blest,
Of this there couldn't be a shadow of doubt.

BARBARA

The fact that his flesh was weaker
Than even Aunt Mary guessed
Took even *her* some time to figure out.

JAMIE

In all these languid latitudes
The atmosphere's exotic

BARBARA

To take up moral attitudes
Would be too idiotic.

JAMIE

Though nobody could be meeker
Than Uncle had been before,

BARBARA

I'll bet today
He's giving 'way

BOTH
At practically every pore.

BOTH
Poor Uncle Harry
BARBARA
Having become a missionary
Found the natives' morals rather crude.
JAMIE
He
BARBARA
And Aunt Mary—
JAMIE
Swiftly imposed an arbitrary
Ban upon them shopping in the nude.
BARBARA
They all considered this silly,
They didn't take it well,
JAMIE
They burnt his boots and several suits
And wrecked the mission hotel.
BARBARA
They also burnt his Mackintosh—
Which made a *disgusting* smell.

BOTH
Poor Uncle Harry
BARBARA
After some words with dear Aunt Mary,
Called upon the chiefs for a pow-wow.
JAMIE
Now they didn't brandish knives at him,
They really were awfully sweet

BARBARA

They made concerted dives at him
And offered him things to eat

JAMIE

But when they threw their wives at him
He had to admit defeat.

BOTH

Uncle Harry's not a missionary now.

The music slows. BARBARA *and* JAMIE *look suddenly serious.*
(*Spoken to Music*)

BARBARA

Poor dear Aunt Mary
Though it was revolutionary
Thought her time had come to take a bow.

JAMIE

Poor Uncle Harry looked at her,
In whom he had placed his trust,
His very last illusion broke
And crumbled away to dust
For she placed a flower behind each[28] ear
And, frankly,
Exposed her bust. (*Pause*)

(*Sung*)

BOTH

Uncle Harry's not a missionary now—

BARBARA

He's left the island

BOTH

But he's certainly not a missionary now.

They cakewalk off as the lights fade.

28

The Music Hall

"Introduction"
(from *The Noël Coward Song Book*)

RODERICK *speaks to the audience.*

"I was born," wrote Noël Coward, "into a world that took light music seriously. The lyrics and melodies of the Edwardian era were hummed and strummed into my consciousness from an early age. My mother played them, my father sang them—my nurse Emma breathed them through her teeth, while she was washing me and putting me to bed. My uncles and aunts, who were legion, sang them singly and in unison, at the slightest provocation."[29]

I'm afraid it's the same with us.

Ladies and gentlemen, may we now present
A Noël Coward Music Hall!

The stage lights up. The curtains open, revealing a turn-of-the-century setting. The medley is sung and danced on the full stage by BARBARA, RODERICK, *and* JAMIE. *Their costumes have been adapted to suggest the 'Nineties.* BARBARA *wears a bustle and carries a parasol. The gentlemen sport boaters and canes.*

"Chase Me, Charlie" (from ACE OF CLUBS)

BARBARA
Chase me, Charlie,
Chase me, Charlie,
Over the garden wall?
I'd like to wander for miles and miles
Wreathed in smiles
Out on the tiles with you.
Chase me, Charlie,
Chase me, Charlie,
Don't be afraid to fall,
Love in the moonlight can be sublime,
Now's the time,
Charlie, I'm
Waiting for you[30]
If you'll only climb
Over the garden wall.

"Saturday Night at the Rose and Crown" (from THE GIRL WHO CAME TO SUPPER)

BARBARA, RODERICK, *and* JAMIE
Saturday night at the Rose and Crown,
Is just the place to be,
Tinkers and Tailors
And Soldiers and Sailors
All out for a bit of a spree,
If you find that you're
Weary of life

With your trouble and strife
And the kids have got you down
It will all come right
On Saturday night
At the Rose and Crown.

"The Island of Bolamazoo" (from OPERETTE)

JAMIE

On the Island of Bolamazoo
Life is almost too good to be true.
You can fish on a reef
Wearing pearls and a leaf
Which at Brighton you never could do.
You don't have to care what the neighbors might think
If some charming young lady should give you a wink—
You can buy her, outright for the price of a drink . . .

ALL

On the Island of Bolamazoo.[31]

"What Ho, Mrs. Brisket"
(from THE GIRL WHO CAME TO SUPPER)

RODERICK

What ho, Mrs. Brisket,
Why not take a plunge and risk it?
The water's warm,
There ain't no crabs
And you'll have a lot of fun among the shrimps and dabs,

If for a lark some saucy old shark
Takes a nibble at your chocolate biscuit
    ALL
Whoo!
    RODERICK
Swim for the shore
And the crowd will roar,
    ALL
What ho, Mrs. Brisket!

    ALL
What ho, Mrs. Brisket,
Why not take a plunge and risk it?
The water's warm,
There ain't no crabs
And you'll have a lot of fun among the shrimps and dabs,
If for a lark
Some saucy old shark
Takes a nibble at your chocolate biscuit—whoo!
Swim for the shore
And the crowd will roar,
What ho, Mrs. Brisket!
Tiddle—iddle—om—pom—tiddle—iddle—om—pom
Pom—tiddly—om—pom
Pom—pom[32]

"Has Anybody Seen Our Ship?"
(from "Red Peppers"—TONIGHT AT 8:30)

    ALL
Has anybody seen our ship?
The *H.M.S. Disgusting.*

We've been on shore
For a month or more
And when we see the captain we shall get 'what for.'
Heave ho, me hearties
The quarterdeck needs dusting.

JAMIE

We had a binge last Christmas year,

RODERICK

Nice plum puddings and a round of beer,

JAMIE

But the captain pulled his cracker and we cried,
Oh dear!

ALL

Has anybody seen—
Has anybody seen—
Has anybody seen our ship?
Oi![33]

They strike a pose. Break for applause.

"Men about Town" (from "Red Peppers"— TONIGHT AT 8:30)

The gentlemen tip their hats to BARBARA, *who exits.*

RODERICK

As . . .

JAMIE

We . . .

BOTH

Stroll down Picc-Piccadilly
In the bright morning air,
All the girls turn and stare,

JAMIE

We're so non—

RODERICK

—chalant

BOTH

And frightfully debonair.
As[34] we chat to Rose, Maud, or Lily
You should see the way their boy friends frown,
For they know without a doubt
That their luck's right out,
Up against a couple of men about town.

BOTH

As we doff hats, each pretty filly
Gives a wink at us and then looks down
For they long with all their might
For a red-hot night
When they see a couple of men about.
See a couple of men about . . .
See a couple of men about town!

Big musical finish. Blackout.

If Love Were All

"If Love Were All" (from BITTER SWEET)

The lights fade up slowly on BARBARA. *The Music Hall setting is still dimly in the background.* BARBARA *has changed back to her original costume, but still carries the hat she wore in the previous section. She moves slowly towards the audience and sings . . .*

Life is very rough and tumble,
For a humble
Diseuse,
One can betray her troubles never,
Whatever
Occurs,
Though I never really grumble
Life's a jumble.
Indeed—
And in my efforts to succeed
I've had to formulate a creed—

I believe in doing what I can,
In crying when I must,

In laughing when I choose.
Heigho, if love were all
I should be lonely,
I believe the more you love a man,
The more you give your trust,
The more you're bound to lose.
Although when shadows fall
I think if only—
Somebody splendid really needed me,
Someone affectionate and dear,
Cares would be ended if I knew that he
Wanted to have me near.
But I believe that since my life began
The most I've had is just
A talent to amuse.
Heigho, if love were all . . .
Heigho, if love were all.

She stands, motionless. The lights slowly fade round her.

Travel

"Too Early or Too Late"
(from a *Holiday* magazine interview)

RODERICK
"My passion for travel," said Noël Coward,
"Has remained undimmed throughout the years;
However, I'm always too early or too late.
I arrive in Japan—
Just when the cherry blossoms have gone.
I arrive in China—
Just before the next revolution.
I ride the Golden Road to Samarkand—
But it's summer and it stinks.
People are always telling me
About something I've just missed . . .
I find this very, very (*Pause*)
Restful."[35]

Blackout.

"Why Do the Wrong People Travel?"
(from SAIL AWAY)

BARBARA and JAMIE are discovered, sitting comfortably on chairs. She is knitting; he is reading the National Geographic *magazine. Music plays quietly under the dialogue.* (*Spoken*)

JAMIE
Travel they say improves the mind,

BARBARA
An irritating platitude
And frankly, entre nous,
Very far from true.

JAMIE
Personally I've yet to find
That longitude and latitude
Can educate those scores
Of monumental bores

BARBARA
There isn't a rock
Between Bangkok
And the beaches of Hispaniola,

JAMIE
That does not recoil
From suntan oil

BARBARA
And the gurgle of Coca-Cola.

The music brightens. They sing.

BOTH

Why do the wrong people travel, travel, travel,
When the right people stay back home?

BARBARA

What compulsion compels them?

JAMIE

And who the hell tells them
To drag their cans to Zanzibar
Instead of staying quietly in Omaha?

BARBARA

In the smallest street
Where the gourmets meet
They invariably fetch up

JAMIE

And it's hard to make
Them accept a steak
That isn't served burned[36] and smeared with ketchup

BARBARA

Please do not think that we criticise or cavil

BOTH

At a genuine urge to roam
But why oh why do the wrong people travel
When the right people stay back home

BARBARA

Send out for pizza[37]

BOTH

When the right people stay back home

JAMIE

Let's have some spare ribs[38]

BOTH

When the right people stay back home.

BOTH

Why do the wrong people travel, travel, travel,
When the right people stay back home?

JAMIE

What explains this mass mania
To leave Pennsylvania
And clack about[39] like flocks of geese

BARBARA

Demanding dry martinis on the isles of Greece!

JAMIE

They will take a train

BARBARA

Or an aeroplane

JAMIE

For an hour on the Costa Brava

BARBARA

And they'll see Pompeii
On the only day
That it's up to its ass in molten lava.

JAMIE

Millions of tourists are churning up the gravel
As they gaze at St. Peter's dome

BOTH

But why oh why do the wrong people travel
When the right people stay back home

JAMIE

Let's have chop suey[40]

BOTH

When the right people stay back home

BARBARA

With lots of egg rolls[41]

BOTH

When the right people stay back home

We're merely asking
When the right people
Stay—back—home.
(Yeah!)[42]

Big musical finish. Blackout

"The Passenger's Always Right"
   (from Sail Away)

RODERICK *is discovered downstage, wearing a naval officer's*
cap.
(*Spoken*)

     RODERICK
When you take a trip
On a boat or ship
Look carefully around you
For ravening hordes
Of smiling frauds
Are certain to surround you.

BARBARA *and* JAMIE *enter, also wearing caps.*

We're off to sea today!
     ALL
Hooray! Hooray! Hooray![43]
     RODERICK
Smiles![44]
     BARBARA
Grace![45]
     JAMIE
Charm!
     ALL
Tact!

RODERICK

We never forget
One vital fact:

(*Sung*)

ALL

The passenger's always right, my boys
The passenger's always right.

JAMIE

The son of a bitch is probably rich
So smile with all your might

BARBARA

Agree to his suggestions.

RODERICK

However coarse or crude,

JAMIE

Reply to all his questions,

RODERICK

Ply him with drink—

BARBARA

Stuff him with food.

RODERICK

The passenger may be sober, boys,

BARBARA

The passenger may be tight,

JAMIE

He may have a yen for raw recruits

RODERICK

Or mountain goats

BARBARA

Or football boots,

JAMIE

But smooth him,

RODERICK

Soothe him,

ALL

Pander to him morning, noon, and night,
The passenger's always right.

ALL

The passenger's always right, my boys,
The passenger's always right.

RODERICK

He may pay a price for curious vice

JAMIE

Or merely want a fight.

BARBARA

He may have inhibitions,

JAMIE

And yearn for secret joys,

RODERICK

Obey your intuitions,

JAMIE

Offer him girls!

BARBARA

Offer him boys!

JAMIE

The passenger may be dumb, my boys,

RODERICK

Or terribly erudite,

BARBARA

Perhaps you can satisfy his needs
With strings of rather nasty beads,

ALL

Compel him,
Sell him

Anything from sex to dynamite.
Remember, boys
The God-damned passenger's always right![46]

They march off into the wings as the lights fade.

Mrs. Worthington

"Mrs. Worthington" (1935)

RODERICK, BARBARA *and* JAMIE *enter separately through the curtains. Their attention is directed to an (apparently) specific person at the back of the auditorium. They sing slowly and politely.*

  RODERICK (*Entering*)
Don't put your daughter on the stage, Mrs. Worthington
  JAMIE (*Entering*)
Don't put your daughter on the stage.
  BARBARA (*Entering*)
She's a bit of an ugly duckling
You must honestly confess,
  RODERICK
And the width of her seat
Would surely defeat
Her chances of success,
  JAMIE
It's a loud voice, and though it's not exactly flat
She'll need a little more than that

To earn a living wage.
On my knees,
Mrs. Worthington

(*Sung*)

ALL
Please,
Mrs. Worthington
Don't put your daughter on the stage.

They move together and sing a little more anxiously.

ALL
Don't put your daughter on the stage, Mrs. Worthington,
Don't put your daughter on the stage,

BARBARA
Though they said at the school of acting
She was lovely as Peer Gynt

RODERICK
I'm afraid on the whole
An ingénue role
Would emphasize her squint,

JAMIE
She's a *big* girl, and though her teeth are fairly good
She's not the type I ever would
Be eager to engage,
No more buts, Mrs. Worthington

ALL
Nuts,
Mrs. Worthington
Don't put your daughter on the stage.

They lose their tempers and scream at her.

ALL

Don't put your daughter on the stage, Mrs. Worthington
Don't put your daughter on the stage.

BARBARA

One look at her bandy legs should prove
She doesn't stand a chance,

RODERICK

In addition to which
The son of a bitch
Can neither sing nor dance,

JAMIE

She's a vile girl and uglier than mortal sin,
The thought of her has put me in[47]
A tearing bloody rage,
That sufficed,
Mrs. Worthington,

ALL

Christ!
Mrs. Worthington,
Don't put your daughter on the stage.

They storm off the stage. Blackout.

Act Two

Mad Dogs and Englishmen

"Mad Dogs and Englishmen"
   (from THE THIRD LITTLE SHOW and WORDS
   AND MUSIC)

The Company has changed into elegant evening dress for the Second Act. For this number BARBARA *carries a lorgnette, with smoked glass.* RODERICK *and* JAMIE *carry tropical fans. They sing with extreme poise and self-confidence.*

   JAMIE
In tropical climes there are certain times of day
When all the citizens retire
To tear their clothes off and perspire.
   BARBARA
It's one of those rules the greatest fools obey,
Because the sun is much too sultry
And one must avoid its ultra-violet ray.
   RODERICK
The natives grieve when the white men leave their huts,
Because they're obviously definitely *nuts!*

51

ALL

Mad dogs and Englishmen
Go out in the midday sun,

RODERICK

The Japanese don't care to.

JAMIE

The Chinese wouldn't dare to.

BARBARA

Hindoos and Argentines sleep firmly from twelve to one.

RODERICK

But Englishmen detest a siesta.

JAMIE

In the Philippines
There are lovely screens
To protect you from the glare.

BARBARA

In the Malay States
There are hats like plates
Which the Britishers won't wear.

RODERICK

At twelve noon
The natives swoon
And no further work is done.

ALL

But mad dogs and Englishmen
Go out in the midday sun.

The gentlemen exchange positions.

JAMIE

It's such a surprise for the Eastern eyes to see
That though the English are effete,
They're quite impervious to heat.

52

BARBARA

When the white man rides every native hides in glee,
Because the simple creatures hope he
Will impale his solar topee on a tree.

RODERICK

It seems such a shame
When the English claim
The earth
That they give rise to such hilarity and mirth.

ALL

Ha—Ha—Ha
Mad dogs and Englishmen
Go out in the midday sun.

JAMIE

The toughest Burmese bandit
Can never understand it.

BARBARA

In Rangoon the heat of noon
Is just what the natives shun.

RODERICK

They put their scotch or rye down
And lie down.

JAMIE

In a jungle town
Where the sun beats down
To the rage of man and beast

BARBARA

The English garb
Of the English sahib
Merely gets a bit more creased.

RODERICK

In Bangkok,

At twelve o'clock
They foam at the mouth and run
ALL
But mad dogs and Englishmen
Go out in the midday sun.

ALL
Mad dogs and Englishmen
Go out in the midday sun:
JAMIE
The smallest Malay rabbit
Deplores this stupid habit.
BARBARA
In Hong Kong
They strike a gong
And fire off a noonday gun
RODERICK
To reprimand each inmate
Who's in late.
JAMIE
In the mangrove swamps
Where the python romps
There is peace from twelve till two.
BARBARA
Even caribous
Lie around and snooze
There's nothing else to do.
RODERICK
In Bengal
To move at all
Is seldom, if ever done,
ALL
But mad dogs and Englishmen

(The music begins to quicken)

Go out in the midday—
Out in the midday—
Out in the midday—
Out in the midday—
Out in the midday—
Out in the midday—
Out in the midday sun!

The music ends very fast and very loud. The company expresses polite dismay, as the lights fade.

A Marvellous Party

"I've Been to a Marvellous Party" (from SET TO MUSIC)

RODERICK *is discovered, seated, clutching a Bloody Mary as if his life depended on it. As the stage brightens, he recoils from the light, but eventually turns and talks to the audience.*

As the number progresses, and the drink is sipped, his mood gradually changes from deep remorse to unbridled hilarity. In the background, throughout, a cocktail piano plays quietly "The Party's Over Now."

(*Also from* SET TO MUSIC)

I have[1] been to a marvellous party
With Nounou and Nada and Nell,
It was in the fresh air
And we went as we were
And we stayed as we were
Which was Hell.
Dear Grace started singing at midnight
And didn't stop singing till four;

Still, we knew some excitement was bound to begin[2]
When Doris[3] got blind on Dubonnet and gin
And scratched her veneer with a Cartier pin,
I couldn't have liked it more.

I have[4] been to a marvellous party,
I must say the fun was intense,
We all had to do
What the people we knew
Might[5] be doing one hundred years hence.
Dear Cecil arrived wearing armor,
Some shells and a black feather boa,
Poor Millicent wore a surrealist comb
Made of bits of mosaic from St. Peter's in Rome,
But the weight was so great that she had to go home,
I couldn't have liked it more.

I have[6] been to a marvellous party
We didn't start dinner till ten.
And young Bobby Carr
Did a stunt at the bar
With a lot of extraordinary men.
Dear Baba arrived with a turtle
Which shattered us all to the core.
The Grand Duke was boring the hell out of Bea[7]
When suddenly Cyril cried[8] "Fiddledidee!"
And ripped off his trousers and jumped in the sea,
I couldn't have liked it more.

I have[9] been to a marvellous party
Elise made an entrance with May,
You'd never have guessed
From her fisherman's vest

That her bust had been *whittled* away.
Poor Lulu got fried on Chianti
And talked about esprit de corps.
Maurice made a couple of passes at Gus
But Billy[10] who hates any kind of a fuss,
Did half the Big Apple and twisted his truss,
I couldn't have liked it more.

We talked about growing old gracefully
And Elsie, who's seventy-four,
Said A: It's a question of being sincere,
And B: If you're supple, you've nothing to fear.
Then she swung upside down from a glass chandelier,
I couldn't have liked it more.

(*The lights begin to fade and the music swells*)

As a matter of fact, it was the most *divine* party I've been to in *weeks,* and Nounou and Nada and Nell are all coming round later and we're going off to *another* party and I just hope it's as *marvellous* as the party we went to last night, because it was *the* most *marvellous* party I have ever been to in my *entire* life . . .

The music drowns the rest of the speech and the lights fade.

Design for Dancing

(Dialogue adapted from: PRIVATE LIVES,
  DESIGN FOR LIVING, SHADOW PLAY, NUDE
  WITH VIOLIN, THE YOUNG IDEA. Music:
  "Dance Little Lady" from THIS YEAR OF
  GRACE!)

BARBARA *is discovered in a vaguely Art Deco pose, with a
large white ostrich feather fan. The orchestra plays the*
Dance Little Lady *theme. The mood throughout is cool.
The music starts to fade into the background and* BARBARA
relaxes from the pose. JAMIE *enters casually from upstage
and arrives at a position slightly to* BARBARA*'s right. They
do not look at one another. After a pause . . .*

JAMIE
Are you engaged for this dance?

BARBARA
I was—but my partner was suddenly taken ill.

JAMIE
It's this damned smallpox epidemic.

BARBARA
No, as a matter of fact it was kidney trouble.

JAMIE

You'll dance it with me, I hope?

BARBARA

I shall be charmed.

They move casually into a formal dance position and, as the music picks up the theme of Dance Little Lady, *they execute a pattern of strange, slow, elegant steps. During which . . .*

BARBARA

Have you ever crossed the Sahara, on a camel?

JAMIE (*After serious thought*)

Frequently. When I was a boy, we used to do it all the time.

They move back to their original positions. The music fades into the background.

RODERICK *enters casually from upstage and arrives at a position slightly to* BARBARA's *left. They do not look at one another. After a pause . . .*

BARBARA

What do you do?

RODERICK (*Pleasantly*)

I work in a bank.

BARBARA

High up in a bank? Or just sitting in a cage, totting up things?

RODERICK

Quite high up really. It's a very good bank.

BARBARA

I'm so glad.

They move gracefully into a close dance position and the Dance Little Lady *theme is repeated. For a while, they sway to the music: their feet do not leave the ground.*

RODERICK

Quite a good floor, isn't it?

BARBARA

I think it needs a little Borax.

RODERICK

I love Borax.

They move through a slow dance pattern, as before. During which . . .

BARBARA

I think life is for living, don't you?

RODERICK

It's difficult to know what else you'd do with it.

They resume their original positions. The music fades again into the background.

BARBARA

Delightful parties Lady Bundle always gives, doesn't she?

RODERICK

Entrancing. Such a dear old lady.

JAMIE

And so gay. Did you notice her at supper—blowing all those shrimps through her ear trumpet?

Pause. BARBARA's *eyes focus somewhere to the right.*

BARBARA

Delicious looking ham on the supper table.

The men's eyes pick out the same spot.

RODERICK

Yes. She has it specially sent from Scotland.

BARBARA

Why Scotland?

RODERICK

It lives there when it's alive.

Pause. BARBARA's *eyes focus somewhere to the left.*

BARBARA

Is that the Grand Duchess Olga, lying under the piano?

The men's eyes pick out the same spot.

JAMIE

Yes. Her husband died a few weeks ago, on his way back from Pulborough.

BARBARA

What on earth was he doing in Pulborough?

JAMIE

Nobody knows exactly: but there have been the usual rumors.

BARBARA

I see.

BARBARA *and* JAMIE's *eyes face front.* RODERICK *continues to peer at the Grand Duchess.*

RODERICK

I lent that woman the top of my thermos flask. And she never returned it. She's shallow, that's what she is, shallow.

The orchestra strikes up the Dance Little Lady *theme yet again. The three heads turn in that direction and they glare at the conductor.*

JAMIE

That orchestra has a remarkably small repertoire.

BARBARA

They don't seem to know anything but this, do they?

They all face front again. After a pause . . .

RODERICK

Are you engaged for this dance?

BARBARA

I was, but my partner was suddenly taken ill.

RODERICK

It's this damned smallpox epidemic.

BARBARA

As a matter of fact, it was kidney trouble.

RODERICK

You'll dance it with me, I hope.

BARBARA

I shall be charmed.

BARBARA *and* RODERICK *go through the motions of the dance, as before. During which . . .*

BARBARA

That hedge over there is called *cupressus macrocapa.*

RODERICK (*Looking*)

Do you swear to it?

BARBARA *glides over to dance with* JAMIE.

JAMIE

Strange how potent cheap music is.

JAMIE *drifts off.* BARBARA *glides over to* RODERICK, *they turn once and he also drifts off.*

The Dance Little Lady *theme begins to dwindle.*

BARBARA *looks at the audience with a strange half-smile— then resumes her original Art Deco pose.*

The music fades completely and the lights dim.

You Were There

"You Were There" (from "Shadow Play"—
   TONIGHT AT 8:30)

     JAMIE (*Entering, in mysterious lighting*)
Was it in the real world
Or was it in a dream?
Was it just a note from some eternal theme
Was it accidental
Or accurately planned?
How could I hesitate
Knowing that my fate
Led me by the hand?

You were there
I saw you and my heart stopped beating
You were there
And in that first enchanted meeting
Life changed its tune,
The stars, the moon
Came near to me.
Dreams that I dreamed

Like magic seemed
To be clear to me, dear to me.
You were there
Your eyes looked into mine and faltered.
Everywhere
The color of the whole world altered.
False became true,
My universe tumbled in two
The earth became heaven for you
Were there.

The lights fade very slowly.

Theatre

"Three White Feathers" (from Words and Music)

BARBARA *and* RODERICK *are seated as if in the back seat of a limousine.* RODERICK *wears some military ribbons.* BARBARA *wears a short white cape, white gloves and a head-dress of three white ostrich plumes. She is very nervous. He is maddeningly calm.*

BARBARA (*Spoken. After a long pause*)
This car hasn't moved in one and three-quarter hours.

RODERICK
I know.

BARBARA
Couldn't we sneak out and slip in the back way?

RODERICK
I don't believe there is a back way into Buckingham Palace.

BARBARA
There must be—they'd never take the groceries past those sentries.

RODERICK (*After a pause*)
I can't understand your being so nervous.

66

BARBARA

Nervous? I'm petrified—being presented to the Queen of England . . . I'd rather face a Monday night audience at the end of the pier.

RODERICK

Relax, darling, just relax.

BARBARA

Relax, how can I relax with all those people gaping at me?

RODERICK

Well, it'll soon be over.

BARBARA (*Looking off*)

That woman in the red hat is laughing at me.

RODERICK (*Also looking*)

Pay no attention.

BARBARA (*Looking out the window*)

Well, you just go right ahead and have yourself a good look. (*Shouting*) Enjoy yourself while you're at it!

RODERICK (*Scandalized*)

Darling, please!

BARBARA (*Abashed*)

I'm sorry . . . but you'd think they'd have something better to do.

RODERICK

You really must try to be a little more dignified.

BARBARA

Dignified? With these three white feathers stuck in my head?—I feel like one of the horses in *Cinderella*.

RODERICK

Just keep calm.

BARBARA

Calm? Oh, that's all very well for you. You were brought up to this—but here I am, a dancing soubrette for fifteen

67

years, being shoved on the palace scene without a rehearsal . . .

RODERICK

Darling, please try to forget the theatre for a little.

BARBARA (*Dramatically*)

That is all I have to remember. That and father's pawn shop. Oh, this isn't my cup of tea, and I believe they all know it . . .[11]

The music starts.

BARBARA (*Speaking to Music*)

I can't help feeling
Fate's made a fool of me rather,
It's placed me where I shouldn't be,
And really couldn't be by rights;
We lived at Ealing,
Me and my mother and father;
I've scaled the social ladder
But I've never had a head for heights;
We had a pawn shop at the corner of the street,
And father did a roaring trade.
I used to think those rings and necklaces were sweet,

(*Sung*)

Now I wouldn't give them to my maid.
I've travelled a long long way
The journey hasn't been all jam;
I must admit
The Rolls in which I sit
Is one up on the dear old tram;
I say to myself each day
In definitely Marble Halls
Today it may be three white feathers,
But yesterday it was three brass balls.

68

I've travelled a long long way
And had a lot of jolts and bumps;
I'll concentrate
And be ahead of fate,
Whichever way the old cat jumps.
I'll wink as I slyly drink
To the ancestors who line our halls,
Today it may be three white feathers,
But yesterday it was three brass—

(*Spoken*)

We're moving!

The music continues quietly in the background.

Oh dear, I don't want to go . . . really I don't . . .

RODERICK

Darling, don't be silly . . . pull yourself together . . . trust me? (*She looks at him*) Trust me. (*Very sincerely*) I think you look very lovely . . . and I'm . . . I'm so very proud of you.[12]

There is a moment between them. Then, with great confidence and poise, she sits up and starts to wave graciously at the imaginary crowds. He smiles at her, and does the same. The music swells and the lights fade.

"The Star"

JAMIE

The newspaper reporter was almost in tears: "Mr. Coward! Mr. Coward!" she cried, "Haven't you *anything* to say to *The Star?*"

"Certainly," said Mr. Coward. "Twinkle."

Blackout.

"The Critic"

RODERICK

The critic was condescending: "Mr. Coward," he said, "I really prefer your acting to your writing."

"Oddly enough," said Mr. Coward, "that's *just* the way I feel about you."

Blackout.

"Epitaph for an Elderly Actress" (from *Not Yet the Dodo* and Other Verses)

BARBARA (*Spoken*)
She got in a rage
About age
And retired, in a huff, from the stage.
Which, taken all round, was a pity
Because she was still fairly pretty
But she got in a rage
About age.

She got in a state
About weight
And resented each morsel she ate.
Her colon she constantly sluiced
And reduced and reduced and reduced
And, at quite an incredible rate
Put on weight.

70

She got in a rage
About age
But she still could have played "Mistress Page"
And she certainly could have done worse
Than *Hay Fever* or "Juliet's Nurse"
But she got in a terrible rage
About age.

And she moaned and she wept and she wailed
And she roared and she ranted and railed
And retired, very heavily veiled,
From the stage.[13]

She drops a deep curtsey and the lights fade.

Love

"Gertie" (from *Present Indicative*)

RODERICK

She was fourteen and I was twelve when I first met her.
We were travelling North together to appear in a morality
play . . . She wore a black satin coat and a black velvet
military cap with a peak. Her face was far from pretty,
but tremendously alive. She was very grown-up, carried a
handbag with a powder puff, and frequently dabbed her
generously turned-up nose.

She confided to me that her name was Gertrude Lawrence, but that I was to call her Gert, because everybody
did. She then gave me an orange, told me a few mildly
dirty stories . . . and I loved her from that moment on-
wards.[14]

The lights cross-fade to . . .

"Loving"

JAMIE
Loving is more important than being in love.
If one can grow from the other, you're all right.
Sometimes it does, sometimes it doesn't;
But when it does—you're in for a long run.

The lights cross-fade to . . .

"I Am No Good at Love"
(from *Not Yet the Dodo* and Other Verses)

RODERICK
I am no good at love
My heart should be wise and free
But I kill the unfortunate golden goose
Whoever it may be
With overarticulate tenderness
And too much intensity.

I am no good at love
I betray it with little sins
For I feel the misery of the end
In the moment it begins
And the bitterness of the last goodbye
Is the bitterness that wins.[15]

The lights cross-fade to . . .

"Sex Talk" (from PRESENT LAUGHTER)

JAMIE

I believe now—and have always believed—that there is far too much nonsense talked about sex. To me, the whole business is vastly overrated. I enjoy it for what it is worth and fully intend going on doing so as long as anybody is interested. And when the time comes that they are not, I shall be perfectly content to settle down with an apple and a good book.[16]

The lights cross-fade to . . .

"A Question of Lighting" (from "Tribute to Marlene Dietrich"—*Not Yet the Dodo* and Other Verses)

RODERICK

We know God made trees
And the birds and the bees
And seas for the fishes to swim in

JAMIE

We are also aware
That he has quite a flair
For creating exceptional women.

RODERICK

When Eve said to Adam,
"Start calling me Madam"
The world became much more exciting

74

Which turns to confusion
The modern delusion
BOTH
That sex is a question of lighting.[17]

Blackout. The gentlemen exit. The curtains open to reveal
BARBARA, *sexily lit.*

"Mad about the Boy" (from WORDS AND MUSIC)

BARBARA (*Spoken to Music*)
I met him at a party just a couple of years ago,
He was rather over-hearty and ridiculous
But as I'd seen him on the Screen
He cast a certain glow[18]
I basked in his attraction for a couple of hours or so,
His manners were a fraction too meticulous,
If he was real or not I couldn't tell

(*Sung*)

But like a silly fool I fell.

Mad about the boy,
It's pretty funny,
But I'm mad about the boy.
I'm quite[19] ashamed of it
But must admit
The sleepless nights I've had about the boy.
Walking down the street
His eyes look out at me
From people that I meet
I can't believe it's true

75

But when I'm blue
In some strange way
I'm glad about the boy.

I'm hardly sentimental
Love isn't so sublime
I have to pay my rental
And I can't afford
To waste much time.
If I could employ
A little magic
That would finally destroy
This dream that pains me
And enchains me
But I can't
Because I'm mad about the boy.

Lord knows I'm not a fool girl
I really shouldn't care
Lord knows I'm not a schoolgirl
In the flurry of her first affair.

Will it ever cloy
This odd diversity of
Misery and joy
I'm feeling quite insane
And young again
And all because I'm
Mad about the boy
Mad about the boy
Mad about the boy.[20]

*The music reaches a great crescendo, then quickly dies.
The lights fade slowly.* BARBARA *remains motionless.*

Women

"Thoughts"

RODERICK

A few years ago, *The National Enquirer* devoted its entire front page to Noël Coward. And there, under a photograph of him—looking no more dapper than usual—came this rather startling headline: "Noël Coward says—'I could take Elizabeth Taylor away from Richard Burton . . . I am the sexiest man alive!'"

Well, as he also remarked, on many other occasions: "It's the thought that counts."

Blackout.

"Nina" (from SIGH NO MORE)

JAMIE (*He wears an exotic, Latin hat*)
Señorita Nina
From Argentina
Knew all the answers

Although her relatives and friends were perfect dancers
She swore she'd never dance a step until she died.
She said, I've seen too many movies
And all they prove is
Too idiotic
They all insist that South America's exotic
Whereas it couldn't be more boring if it tried!

She said that frankly she was blinded
To all their overadvertised romantic charms
And then she got more bloody-minded
And told them where to put their tropic palms.
She said, I hate to be pedantic
But it drives me nearly frantic
When I see that unromantic
Sycophantic
Lot of sluts
For ever wriggling their guts
It drives me absolutely nuts!

She declined[21] to begin the Beguine
When they requested it
And she made an embarrassing scene
If anyone suggested it
For she detested it.
Though no one ever could be keener
Than little Nina
On quite a number
Of very eligible men who did the Rhumba
When they proposed to her she merely left them flat.
She said that love should be impulsive
But not compulsive
And syncopation

Had a discouraging effect on procreation,
And that she'd rather read a book—and that was that!

She refused[22] to begin the Beguine
When[23] they besought her to
And with[24] language profane and obscene
She cursed the man who taught her to
She cursed Cole Porter too!
From this it's fairly clear that Nina
In her demeanor
Was so offensive
That when the hatred of her friends grew too intensive
She thought she'd better beat it while she had the chance.
After some trial and tribulation
She reached the station
And met a sailor
Who had acquired a wooden leg in Venezuela
And so she married him because he *couldn't* dance!

There surely never could have been a
More irritating girl than Nina,
They never speak in Argentina
Of this degenerate bambina
Who had the luck to find romance
And[25] resolutely wouldn't dance.[26]

(*Spoken*)

She wouldn't dance!
Olé!

Blackout.

"Mrs. Wentworth-Brewster" ("A Bar on the Piccola Marina," from NOËL COWARD IN LAS VEGAS)

RODERICK

I'll sing you a song
It's not very long
Its moral may disconcert you,
Of a mother and wife,
Who for most of her life,
Was famed for domestic virtue.
She had two strapping daughters and a rather dull son
And a much duller husband, who at sixty-one,
Elected to retire
And, later on, expire.
Sing Hallelujah
Hey nonny-no, Hey nonny-no, Hey nonny-no!
He joined the feathered choir.
Having laid him to rest
By special request
In the family mausoleum,
As his widow repaired
To the home they had shared,
Her heart sang a gay *Te Deum*.
And then, in the middle of the funeral wake
With her mouth full of excellent Madeira cake[27]
She briskly cried, That's done.
My life's at last begun.
Sing Hallelujah
Hey nonny-no, Hey nonny-no, Hey nonny-no!
It's time I had some fun.

Today, though hardly a jolly day,
At least has set me free,
(Now)[28]
Let's[29] all have a lovely holiday—
On the Island of Capri!
In a bar on the Piccola Marina
Life called to Mrs. Wentworth-Brewster
Fate beckoned her and introduced her
Into a rather queer
Unfamiliar atmosphere.
She'd just sit there, propping up the bar
Beside a fisherman who sang to a guitar.
When accused of having gone too far,
She merely cried, Funiculi!
Just fancy me!
Funicula!
When he bellowed, Che bella signorina!
Sheer ecstasy at once produced a
Wild shriek from Mrs. Wentworth-Brewster
Changing her whole demeanor.
When both her daughters and her son said,
Please come home, Mama.
She answered[30] rather bibulously, Who do you think you
    are?
Nobody can afford to be so lahdy-bloody-da,
In a bar on the Piccola Marina.

Every fisherman cried,
"Viva Viva" and "Che vagazza,"
When she sat on the Grand Piazza
Everybody would rise,
Every fisherman sighed,

"Viva Viva Che bell' Inglesi"
Someone even said "Whoops-a-daisy,"
Which was quite a surprise.
Each evening with some light excuse[31]
And beaming with goodwill,
She'd just slip into something loose
And totter down the hill.

To that bar on the Piccola Marina
Where love came to Mrs. Wentworth-Brewster,
Hot flushes of delight suffused her
Right round the bend she went
Picture her astonishment
Day in, day out she would gad about
Because she felt she was no longer on the shelf.
Night out, night in, knocking back the gin,
She cried, "Hurrah
Funiculi
Funicula
Funic yourself!"

(*Sung*)

Just for fun three young sailors from Messina
Bowed low to Mrs. Wentworth-Brewster,
Said Scusi and abruptly[32] goosed her.
Then there was quite a scena.
Her family, in floods of tears, cried,
Leave these men, Mama.
She said, "Why? . . .[33]
I mean,[34]
They're just high-spirited,
Like all Italians are—

82

And most of them have a great deal more
To offer than Papa . . ."
In a bar
On the Piccola Marina.

Blackout.

World Weary

"World Weary" (from THIS YEAR OF GRACE!)

BARBARA *is discovered, swathed in maribou, in dramatic low-key lighting.*

BARBARA
When I'm feeling dreary and blue
I'm only too
Glad to be left alone,
Dreaming of a place in the sun.
When day is done,
Far from the[35] telephone;
Because I'm world weary, world weary
Living in a great big town,
I find it so dreary, so dreary,
Everything looks grey or brown,
RODERICK (*Entering*)
I want an ocean blue,
JAMIE (*Entering*)
Great big trees,

84

BARBARA

A bird's-eye view
Of the Pyrenees,

ALL

We want to watch the moon rise up
And see the great red sun go down
Watching clouds go by
Through a Wintry sky
Fascinates us
But when we're standing in the street[36]
Every cop we meet
Simply hates us,
Because we're world weary, world weary,
We could kiss the railroad tracks,
We want to get right back to nature
Assume a horizontal stature[37]
We want to get right back to nature—
And
Relax . . .

On this last word, the orchestra suddenly erupts into a very loud jazz pattern. The stage lights brighten. The cast looks uncertain for a moment, then proceeds.

Let's Do It

"Let's Do It" (Music by Cole Porter.
  Lyrics adapted by Noël Coward and
  Roderick Cook)

BARBARA, RODERICK *and* JAMIE *address the audience.*

RODERICK
Mr. Irving Berlin
Often emphasizes sin
In a charming way.

BARBARA
Noël Coward we know
Wrote a song or two to show
That sex was here to stay.

JAMIE
Richard Rodgers it's true
Took a more romantic view
Of this sly, biological urge.

RODERICK
But it really was Cole—
Who contrived to make the whole
Thing merge.

86

BARBARA

He said that Belgians and Greeks do it

JAMIE

Nice young men who sell antiques do it,

ALL

Let's do it, let's fall in love.

RODERICK

In Texas some of the men do it

BARBARA

Others drill a hole and then do it

ALL

Let's do it, let's fall in love.

RODERICK

E. Allan Poe—ho ho ho—did it
But he did it in verse,

JAMIE

H. Beecher Stowe did it
But she had to rehearse

RODERICK

Aretha Franklin with soul does it,

BARBARA

Julia Child in a casserole does it,

ALL

Let's do it, let's fall in love.

JAMIE

Miss America, under the flag, does it,

BARBARA

The man from Glad with a little bag does it,

ALL

Let's do it, let's fall in love.

RODERICK
The Royal Ballet to a man do it,
JAMIE
Tinkerbell and Peter Pan do it,
ALL
Let's do it, let's fall in love.

BARBARA
Each Miss Gabor time and again does it—
They keep trying, God knows
RODERICK
Lawrence Welk with champagne does it
But the bubbles get up his nose,
BARBARA
They say that every hormone does it,
JAMIE
Mr. Portnoy all alone does it,
ALL
Let's do it, let's fall in love.

BARBARA
Miss Doris Day won't do it
She thinks it offends . . . (*Exits*)

JAMIE
Ferrante and Teicher don't do it
They're just very good friends . . . (*Exits*)

RODERICK
Snow White felt that she must do it
Seven Dwarfs could only ju-u-ust do it! (*Exits*)

Big musical finish. Blackout.

Finale

The full stage is romantically lit.
BARBARA, JAMIE, *and* RODERICK *sing in separate spots.*

"Where Are the Songs We Sung?" (from OPERETTE)

JAMIE
Where are the songs we sung
When love in our hearts was young?
Where in the limbo of the swiftly passing years,
Lie all our hopes and dreams, and fears . . .

"Someday I'll Find You" (from PRIVATE LIVES)

RODERICK
Someday I'll find you,
Moonlight behind you,
True to the dream I am dreaming
As I draw near you,

You'll smile a little smile;
For a little while
We shall stand
Hand in hand . . .

"I'll Follow My Secret Heart"
   (from CONVERSATION PIECE)

BARBARA

I'll follow my secret heart
My whole life through,
I'll keep all my dreams apart
Till one comes true.
No matter what price is paid,
What stars may fade
Above,
I'll follow my secret heart
Till I find love . . .

"If Love Were All" (from BITTER SWEET)

RODERICK

For[38] I believe . . .

RODERICK *and* JAMIE

That since my life began . . .

ALL

The most I've had is just
A talent to amuse.
Heigh ho,
If love were all . . .

The music swells. The lights brighten.

"Play, Orchestra, Play" (from "Shadow Play"— Tonight at 8:30)

(*Sung*)

ALL

Play, orchestra, play,
Play something light and sweet and gay
For we must have music
We must have music
To drive our fears away.

JAMIE

While our illusions
Swiftly fade from[39] us,

RODERICK

Let's have an orchestra score

BARBARA

In the confusion
The years have made for us,

ALL

Serenade for us,
Just once more.

(*Very quietly and intently*)

Life needn't be grey.
Although it's changing day by day,
Though a few old dreams may decay
Play,
Orchestra,
Play,
Orchestra,
Play,

Orchestra,
Play . . . !

"I'll See You Again" (from BITTER SWEET)

The lights start to dim, leaving the cast together in one spot.

ALL
Though our world may go awry
Though the years our tears may dry
We shall love you till we die . . .

(*They clasp hands. Spoken*)

JAMIE
Goodbye.

BARBARA
Goodbye.

RODERICK
Goodbye.

The music swells as the lights fade. The cast hovers for a moment in silhouette. The final chords crash out. Darkness.

Source Material for *Oh Coward!*

(The dates indicate the first productions, in London and New York, with names of some of the featured players)

THE YOUNG IDEA (London, Savoy Theatre, 1923. Noël Coward, Herbert Marshall, Kate Cutler)
Dialogue: Design for Dancing
ON WITH THE DANCE (London, London Pavilion, 1925. Hermione Baddeley, Leonide Massine, Alice Delysia)
Poor Little Rich Girl
THIS YEAR OF GRACE! (London, London Pavilion, 1928. Maisie Gay, Jessie Matthews, Sonnie Hale) (New York, Selwyn Theatre, 1928. Noël Coward, Beatrice Lillie, Florence Desmond)
A Room with a View
Dance Little Lady
World Weary
BITTER SWEET (London, His Majesty's Theatre, 1929. Peggy Wood, Georges Metaxa, Ivy St. Helier) (New York, Ziegfeld Theatre, 1929. Evelyn Laye, Gerald Nodin)

I'll See You Again

If Love Were All

Zigeuner

PRIVATE LIVES (London, Phoenix Theatre, 1930, and New York, Times Square Theatre, 1931. Noël Coward, Gertrude Lawrence, Laurence Olivier)

Someday I'll Find You

Dialogue: Design for Dancing

COCHRAN'S 1931 REVUE (London, London Pavilion, 1931. John Mills, Ada-May)

Bright Young People

THE THIRD LITTLE SHOW (New York, Music Box Theatre, 1931. Beatrice Lillie)

Mad Dogs and Englishmen

WORDS AND MUSIC (London, Adelphi Theatre, 1932. Ivy St. Helier, John Mills, Joyce Barbour, Romney Brent, Doris Hare)

Something to Do with Spring

Let's Say Goodbye

Mad about the Boy

Three White Feathers

The Party's Over Now

Mad Dogs and Englishmen

DESIGN FOR LIVING (New York, Ethel Barrymore Theatre, 1933. Noël Coward, Lynn Fontanne, Alfred Lunt) (London, Haymarket Theatre, 1939. Anton Walbrook, Diana Wynyard, Rex Harrison)

Dialogue: Design for Dancing

CONVERSATION PIECE (London, His Majesty's Theatre, 1934, and New York, 44th Street Theatre, 1934. Noël Coward, Yvonne Printemps, Irene Browne. Pierre Fresnay played Sir Noël's part in New York)

I'll Follow My Secret Heart

TONIGHT AT 8.30 (London, Phoenix Theatre, 1936, New York, National Theatre, 1936. Noël Coward, Gertrude Lawrence, Joyce Carey, Alan Webb)

Play, Orchestra, Play   from "Shadow Play"

You Were There   from "Shadow Play"

Dialogue: Design for Dancing   from "Shadow Play"

We Were Dancing   from "We Were Dancing"

Has Anybody Seen Our Ship?   from "Red Peppers"

Men about Town   from "Red Peppers"

OPERETTE (London, His Majesty's Theatre, 1938. Peggy Wood, Fritzi Massary, Irene Vanbrugh)

The Island of Bolamazoo

The Stately Homes of England

Where Are the Songs We Sung?

SET TO MUSIC (New York, Music Box Theatre, 1939. Beatrice Lillie, Richard Haydn)

I've Been to a Marvellous Party

PRESENT LAUGHTER (London, Haymarket Theatre, 1943. Noël Coward, Judy Campbell, James Donald) (New York, Plymouth Theatre, 1946. Clifton Webb, Jan Sterling)

Sex Talk

UP AND DOING (London, Saville Theatre, 1940. Binnie Hale)

London Pride

SIGH NO MORE (London, Piccadilly Theatre, 1945. Cyril Ritchard, Madge Elliott, Graham Payn, Joyce Grenfell)

That Is the End of the News

Nina

PACIFIC 1860 (London, Drury Lane Theatre, 1946. Mary Martin, Graham Payn)

Uncle Harry

This Is a Changing World

ACE OF CLUBS (London, Cambridge Theatre, 1950. Pat Kirkwood, Graham Payn)

Sail Away

Chase Me, Charlie

NOËL COWARD IN LAS VEGAS (Cabaret, The Desert Inn, 1955. Noël Coward, Peter Matz, and Orchestra)

Uncle Harry (new lyrics)

A Bar on the Piccola Marina

NUDE WITH VIOLIN (London, Globe Theatre, 1956. John Gielgud, Joyce Carey, Kathleen Harrison) (New York, Belasco Theatre, 1957. Noël Coward, Joyce Carey, Mona Wasbourne)

Dialogue: Design for Dancing

SAIL AWAY (New York, Broadhurst Theatre, 1961. London, Savoy Theatre, 1962. Elaine Stritch, Grover Dale)

The Passenger's Always Right

Why Do the Wrong People Travel

THE GIRL WHO CAME TO SUPPER (New York, Broadway Theatre, 1963. José Ferrer, Florence Henderson, Tessie O'Shea, Irene Browne, Roderick Cook)

What Ho, Mrs. Brisket

Saturday Night at the Rose and Crown

Songs not previously used in any musical production

Mrs. Worthington (1935)

We Must All Be Very Kind to Auntie Jessie (circa 1924)

The Noël Coward Song Book (1953)

Music Hall Introduction   from "Introduction"

Present Indicative (Autobiography 1937)

Gertie

Future Indefinite (Autobiography 1954)

The Star

Not Yet the Dodo and Other Verses (Verse 1968)
  The Boy Actor
  I Am No Good at Love
  A Question of Lighting (from Tribute to Marlene
    Dietrich)
Star Quality (*Six Short Stories* 1951)
  London Pastoral   from "Ashes of Roses"
Holiday magazine
  Too Early or Too Late
The National Enquirer (1963)
  Thoughts (Women)
Paris (New York, Music Box Theatre, 1928. Irene Bordoni.
    Words and Music by Cole Porter)
  "Let's Do It" (Additional lyrics by Noël Coward, by kind
    permission of the composer and his estate)

The item known as "The Critic" was told to me by Seymour
Krawitz, and the item called "Loving" I first saw on the
sleeve of an old record album by Carmen Macrae, entitled
"Mad about the Man." My thanks to both.

R.C.

Notes

1. Original Coward lyric "sort"
2. Original Coward lyric "most"
3. Last four lines interpolated for this production
4. Original Coward lyrics rearranged for this production
5. See note 4
6. Original Coward lyrics rearranged for this production
7. See note 6
8. Original Coward lyric "with"
9. Original Coward lyric "seems"
10. Original Coward prose edited and condensed
11. Original Coward dialogue lead-in rewritten for this production
12. Original Coward lyric "had"
13. Original Coward lyric "in trouble"
14. Original Coward lyric line "That hernia she had has turned out to be double,"
15. Original Coward lyric "Percy's"
16. Original Coward lyric "eleven"
17. Original Coward lyrics rearranged for this production
18. Rewritten dialogue for this production
19. Original Coward lyrics rearranged for this production
20. Rewritten dialogue for this production
21. Original Coward lyrics rearranged for this production
22. Original Coward lyric "beat up"
23. Original Coward lyric "unkind"
24. Original Coward lyrics rearranged for this production
25. Original Coward lyric line "My family has traditions"
26. Original Coward lyric line "I've heard them a thousand times"

27. Original Coward lyric "greeted"
28. Original Coward lyric "her"
29. Edited and rewritten for this production
30. Original Coward lyric line "Bound to give in"
31. Lyrics rearranged for this production
32. Last three lines added for this production
33. Lyrics rearranged for this production
34. Original Coward lyric "when"
35. Edited for this production
36. Original Coward lyric "rare"
37. Lyric lines added for this production
38. Same as note 37
39. Original Coward lyric "around"
40. Same as note 37
41. Same as note 37
42. Lyrics for entire song rearranged for this production
43. Spoken introduction added for this production
44. Original Coward lyric "Bow"
45. Original Coward lyric "Smile"
46. Lyrics for entire song rearranged and combined with "The Customer's Always Right" for this production
47. Original Coward lyric line "One look at her has put me in"

Act Two

1. Original Coward lyric "I've"
2. Original Coward lyric line "We knew the excitement was bound to begin"
3. Original Coward lyric "Laura"
4. Original Coward lyric "I've"
5. Original Coward lyric "would"
6. Original Coward lyric "I've"
7. Original Coward lyric line "The Grand Duke was dancing a foxtrot with me"
8. Original Coward lyric "screamed"
9. Original Coward lyric "I've"
10. Original Coward lyric "And Freddie"
11. Original Coward dialogue adapted and changed for this production
12. Original Coward dialogue adapted and changed for this production
13. Original Coward verse condensed for this production
14. Original Coward prose condensed and adapted for this production
15. Original Coward verse condensed for this production
16. Original Coward dialogue adapted for this production
17. Original Coward verse condensed for this production
18. Original Coward lyric "spell"
19. Original Coward lyric "so"

20. Original Coward lyrics rearranged for this production
21. Original Coward lyric "refused"
22. Original Coward lyric "declined"
23. Original Coward lyric "though"
24. Original Coward lyric "in"
25. Original Coward lyric "but"
26. Original Coward lyrics rearranged for this production
27. Original Coward lyric line "While adding some liquor to the Tipsy Cake"
28. Non-Coward lyric "(Now)" added for this production
29. Original Coward lyric "We'll"
30. Original Coward lyric "murmured"
31. Original Coward lyric line "Each night she'd make some gay excuse."
32. Original Coward lyric "politely"
33. Non-Coward lyric "why?" added for this production
34. Non-Coward lyric line "I mean" added for this production
35. Original Coward lyric "a"
36. Original Coward lyrics "But if we do it"
37. Two lyric lines added for this production
38. Original Coward lyric "But"
39. Original Coward lyric "for"